RED

SHOES

RED
SHOES

poems

Honor Moore

W. W. NORTON & COMPANY

NEW YORK   LONDON

For information about permission to reproduce
selections from this book, write to Permissions,
W. W. Norton & Company, Inc., 500 Fifth Avenue,
New York, NY 10110

Manufacturing by Courier Westford
Book design by JAM Design
Production manager: Anna Oler

Library of Congress Cataloging-in-Publication Data

Moore, Honor, 1945–
Red shoes ; poems / Honor Moore.—1st ed.
      p. cm.
Includes bibliographical references.
ISBN 0-393-05985-5 (hardcover)
I. Title.
PS3563.0617R43 2005
811'.54—dc22   2005008062

W. W. Norton & Company, Inc.
500 Fifth Avenue, New York, N.Y. 10110
www.wwnorton.com

W. W. Norton & Company Ltd.
Castle House, 75/76 Wells Street, London W1T 3QT

1 2 3 4 5 6 7 8 9 0

for the man in the dark

CONTENTS

RED

SHOES

I

DISPARU

TANGO

A man crosses a street.
The red glove

Pulls him toward her
Down into him

It's like water falling.
So many years outside

The circle
A ring her mouth would make.

He falls back.
She knows how it would be

He cries out.
She makes him cry out.

AUBADE

The south wind is presented as an eagle
no matter what she does to draw him
as heated sky, open daisy, an elm
where there are no elms.

She wears night gloves to water flowers
that bloom only in the dark, whose
scent rifles her sleep, whose petals close
at the hint of light.

At his gold cry, the rooster's crown
flares: voluminous horizon
window opening, a parade of child soldiers.
This is what she dreamed

before waking, before his feet undid
her bashfulness and day opened like an egg.

HOTEL BRINDISI

The glass door was spinning panes
like an open book.
A suit the color of sky close to night,
wire of eyeglasses a gold moon.

He bowed as if judicial
and called a French name.
Glasses were filled with ice
the color of amber.

We were in America.

He asked me to take his hands.
They are cold, he said.
I warmed his cold hands
as we sat on the rouge banquette.

It was the last May of the century.

His eyes looked at my face.
His hand fell to the glacier
of my thigh and held on.
My gold tail swam dark green water,

the ocean smelled of gardenia.
Outside on the avenue people
scurried to their palaces, wearing
sunglasses, carrying shiny bags.

SUMMER

In her garden birds bewail the singe
of absence. It was almost five,
the brick wall greened by a veil
of moss, artifact of city heat. The dog
noses her face toward
movement of air, half the windows
long dead. As you drove the Hudson,
swans from a promontory,
clouds glowering as your gaze
pulled at the root of the island.
What did we look like talking
money and heartbreak? Fire escapes
zigzag brick, balconies barred
with spiraled iron. Make a note:
Beneath the windows, water
stained the brick. Assume years of
air dulled the color almost white.

HOMAGE

I have straight hair and I wore
Purple tonight and orange
But I saw no man on the street
I could desire, though I looked.

I have one on my bedside table
And a phone, also white plastic
The light on, white lampshade
And a nightgown, white too.

It shimmers under the purple lamp,
I turn it on with a switch.
The sky was so blue today
You could cut it. My hair is straight

But the hair on my pubis curls
After a bath and so does
The telephone cord that dangles
White in the dark.

My night table is mahogany
Its drawers have crystal knobs.
The lamp is glass, its finial brass.
I've kept it a very long time.

FANTASIA

Hours before sun enfolds the city heartbreak
wings a traverse until at my hip it rests

exhaling its dissonant aria, coloratura
diphthongs leaping, dipping, veering

all the way to aspirin. The sky is almost
saturated with color though its center

is blank, something serious and opposite
tipping inward so no one approaches.

We'll stop at the rise in the road where
it all vanishes behind a meadow, ermine

or swaths of green, but I keep track of
green. This is my favorite place, he said,

and I looked out. Oh dear, I've forgotten
to feed you. Someone else takes the baby

as he begins his walk through glass, leaves
darkening, sun raw out evening

windows, the river drowning
as rain sweeps, everything white as if on fire.

This time the rims of his eyes are gold, his
weight almost comforting as he hangs

from my neck like a shawl, ladder of violet
diamonds loosening at last. I'm hungry,

he whispers. I dream an empty bridge,
light restored to the city, a bandstand

spangled with candles, and dressed in azure,
the violinist alone, playing her heart out.

JANUARY LIGHT

January a week gone, and I can tell
Already spring's a glint, almost an idea:
Melt, freeze, melt—slipping, you dip
Even fall as daylight widens and I
Saunter through dusks that lean,
Lurch, break, hallucinating sunshine.
Atmospheric this leap for heat—dizzy raj,
Pasha—snowdrop, crocus, aria
Intent to bless, to heal the maim
North wind has gorged. Oh winter engine
Eke out this dark before your end begins.

THE ROBBERY

The sky turned purple, bright purple
so I wasn't sure if it was real
or part of my dream—the train,
all of us on a train traveling
through the mountains, a strange
landscape, the sky pale, everything
dark against it. Columns, trees
bright green, and then a clock tower
built of brick that resembled ivory,
face gold in the coming
night, baroque horses rampant,
pearlescent beyond the dusky
indigo. I had stolen her jewelry
and now I was willing to return it.
The train stopped beneath the burnished
portico, but only for a moment,
long enough for me to hand
amethysts to the tall bartender
who thanked me in Italian.
Donald lay nearly asleep, refusing
to watch the changing sky or look at
the architecture, gesture of a city
long kept from us. The end of sun
burned the horizon as we ate
around a table the color of violins.

Yes, I remember—horses fearful,
foam at their mouths as they rear;
the clock, enormous; the roofs
verdigris, glittering at moon rise.

Doorway

My hand black

when held up to reluctant—

Lean against me

A walk in the dark.

Here.

I had to stumble—

Hands.

Lean against me

Blues from Bed

The blue cup
Landscape of blue mountain, yellow cloud
Blue bowl on the shell pink shelf
And a blue goat

Blue book at the end of a shelf
On the first day of the new year
A new self
Blue sky out the window, white snow

Sun striping indigo
Blue eye tilted or open
Of love, inadvertent
Lid recedes up cornea like a wave

Sleeving back to blue
Smoothed ripple sheen of ocean
Above a gentian mountain
You are my sky

Blue roof, marks for windows
At the end of the shelf a blue book
Than which no other book
Is as blue, bluer

Than glistery eyeskin
Nearly the turquoise certain days ocean is.
Blue at some distances unblues,
Creeps up beach

Bodies in water or love
Rub of blue glue on a girl's dove.
I like blue and white porcelain
Ginger jar lamp, sugar bowl

Your black eye is actually blue
Loosened blood slid
Blue under pale skin, as a cup
Sky, eye. As blue as up.

New Shoes

She wore them with silk and black sheers,
Her winter legs twin moons under lace—
New shoes, handmade, gleaming, polished
As a lake at twilight or a new mirror:
Fashioned for men, but cut for a woman.
He wanted her, he said, wearing those shoes.

Dreaming as they measure her shoeless,
A cobbler in Florence, his tape shearing
Her foot, no question a woman
Requires such shoes. Wear them with lace,
Signora, offering brush and polish.
The saddle's rough, but the toe will mirror

All he undoes, her each gesture mirror
His guiding one, as she rises in shoes
Made for holding ground, for polished
Floors, for business in suits and sheers.
When I wear them, she muses, will he unlace
And unravel me? Take have and woman

Me? His hands open her skirt, manning
And mixing until her face is his mirror,
Till he seats and unties her, untangling laces,
Loosening, pulling, prizing back shoe

Edge, cherry insoles flushed, he shears
The tongue from each sweat-polished

Instep. Forthright now, as if polishing,
She fingers his face, pale as a woman's
In fugitive streetlight, her hands sheer
Contentment, his eyes closed in the mirror
Hers are. Kick, he says, off with the shoes!
She does, fingers through his like lacing,

And his hand breaks from hers, unlaces
Stocking from garter, quick as a polish
Cloth snapping. Take off *your* shoes,
She says. I want you naked as a woman.
I like hair on shoulders, I like mirrors
When they tangle light. Outside sirens shear

Night as if a swerve of polish could unmirror
Sheer dark, the man and woman whispering
Always wear lace! Do you like my shoes?

U P T O W N

A racket across the planet
actually a parlor

as if he were a dog
handkerchief red as a tongue

keria in bloom, egg yolk
polka dots enameled onto green.

The door is open because it's May.

His jacket was as soft as a rabbit
he was as mine as a dog.

In the park before nine a.m.
you can let dogs loose.

Smiling as if his switch were stuck.

Summer came
blistering like an ambulance.

When the party was over
we all went home.

VIOLETTA, 2000

A black satin purse in her right hand,
condoms, spermicide,
her key to the birdcage elevator.
All night, thunder and rain
in a flash of lightning, his hands visible,
leaves of philodendron, a half-moon table.

They talk in near dark, eating from a basket.
She places her hand in his lap,
opens her legs as if God came from her,
fragrance pluming like smoke.
All night, his tongue like a fish
philodendron green smoothing half-light.

Now the bridge is illuminated, twin
arches rising, chalky, incandescent,
light abandoning the dome of sky,
river breathing azure, its surface frazzled,
the moon leaving her scuff marks.
Near the open window, dark of leaves.

Outside at dawn, the sun hidden,
a crow lowering itself on black wings
crosses before windows as gold as Rome.

The telephone, her mouth open.

I can see all the way into you, he says.

Leaves of philodendron pour from the table.

DISPARU

I spent the day with invisible you, your arms
invisible around me, holding me blue in your
open invisible eyes. We walked invisible,
invisible and happy, daydreaming sight as if
light were a piano it played on. Invisible
my hand at your well-cut trouser, invisible
speeding night, the invisible taxi, bare
the invisible legs, kissing the vanishing
mouths, breasts invisible, your, my invisible
entwining, the sheets white as geese, blue as sky.
And darling, how your invisible prick rose,
rosy, invisible, invisible as all night
galloping, swinging, we tilted and sang.

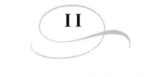

GNOSTIC

Exactly Perpendicular

If I lean into the window and look out toward
Houston Street, I see the church tower where the bell rings
twelve times at noon. Snow is billowing across the sky,
settling on the roof of St. Anthony's Hall, or on the steps that
lead up to the roof of a higher building next door.

The rope pulls away, and a ship sails down my
arm until my hand freezes.

My father in a dream, his penis inside me.

Excuse me, take it out.

Dead of winter in the city. I see sky beyond the low
roof of St. Anthony's Hall, then the concrete back wall of
the tenements that face the street one block west, and to the
north the tar roof of St. Anthony's Church.

Night holds down my chest.

The sky is white, a thick white. Red that was
bright yesterday is dull, and there's a yellow door I haven't
seen before. That's where the steps lead.

In the dream, my lips wobble.

A sheep sails down my arm—

Excuse be, dake it out.

Outside the window is a piece of rope wind knocks
repeatedly against the glass, as if this room were a ship and
the rope a piece of rigging. There's a peeled tangerine on the
radiator. When you bite through the dry skin, juice splashes.
All over.

My father's sister died, and I inherited her silver
pencil sharpener.

When I returned the dagger to my father, he said it
wasn't his. The black blade had a wavy shape. The handle was
made of gold, encrusted with jewels. The hilt was ebony and it
was broken.

My mother dies, and years later, so does my father.

Snow is billowing across the sky, resting on St.
Anthony's roof, or on the steps that lead up to the roof of the
higher building next door. The sky is white. The red is a door
I haven't seen before. That's where the steps lead.

I open the door.

Hello.

I lift my hands to protect my eyes.

The second time, we meet standing.

I tell him I will take the taxi with him.

Rising sun turns the cement reverse of the church façade bright gold, the cement cross brass against the sky which is very blue. As day accumulates, colors become "true." I prefer the "false" colors of twilight and dawn.

Altogether, there were two taxis.

I will never forget the bare polished floors, the French doors, the leather sofa I sat on, holding the phone. Something about the room was blue. Not the walls. The walls were white and the windows were large. Outside was a street, houses set at measured intervals. There was nothing beautiful about the street, but it is there I understood what happened.

There was no penis and there was no blade, but the effect was of cutting. I see the consequences in the clothes I wear in old family photographs, and in the stiffness with which my aunt, my father's sister, held herself as she grew old.

There is a blue door in the concrete wall, and the sun is at an angle that puts the concrete in shadow so it seems to be the color of smoke. The blue door looks exactly perpendicular, as if it is in shadow and not blue at all.

To whom did the dagger belong? I found it in the closet in my father's house, the house where I lived, the house whose roof was torn off.

Outside is a piece of rope the wind knocks repeatedly against the glass, as if this were a ship and the rope a rigging cable. The rope pulls away and the ship sails down my arm, then my hand freezes.

His mouth was fragrant.

Freesia, calla lily, gardenia. All white.

I was hungry.

On the ship I tell him my hands are cold. He takes
them between his, and lifting them to his mouth, breathes on my
fingers and palms.

There is a black-and-white photograph of my aunt
in her wedding dress. She stands tall and impossibly thin,
holding a white bouquet, her long bridal veil swirling around her
feet as if she were rising from the waters of Shalott. Absolutely
beautiful. When she talked about waltzing, you understood what
she believed she had lost.

WALLACE STEVENS

The great poet came to me in a dream, walking toward me in a house
drenched with August light. It was late afternoon and he was old,

past a hundred, but virile, fit, leonine. I loved that my seducer
had lived more than a century and a quarter. What difference

does age make? We began to talk about the making of poems, how
I craved his green cockatoo when I was young, named my Key West

after his, like a parent naming a child "George Washington." He was
not wearing the business suit I'd expected, nor did he have the bored

Rushmore countenance of the familiar portrait. His white tee shirt
was snug over robust chest and belly, his golden hair long, his beard

full as a biker's. How many great poets ride a motorcycle? We
were discussing the limits of image, how impossible for word

to personate entirely thing: "sea," ocean an August afternoon; "elm,"
heartbreak of American boulevards after the slaughter

of sick old beautiful trees. "I have given up language," he said.
The room was crowded and noisy, so I thought I'd misheard.

"Given up words?" "Yes, but not poems," he said, whereupon
he turned away, walking into darkness. Then it was cooler, and

we were alone in the gold room. "Here is a poem," he said, proffering
a dry precisely formed leaf, on it two dead insects I recognized

as termites, next to them a tiny flag of scarlet silk no larger than
the price sticker on an antique brooch. Dusky red, though once

bright, frayed but vivid. Minute replica of a matador's provocation?
Since he could read my spin of association, he was smiling, the glee

of genius. "Yes," he said, "that is the poem." A dead leaf? His grin was
implacable. Dead, my spinner brain continued, but beautiful. Edge

curling, carp-shaped, color of bronze or verdigris. Not one, but two
termites—dead. To the pleasures of dining on sill or floor joist, of

eating a house, and I have sold my house. I think of my friend finding
termites when she reached, shelf suddenly dust on her fingers,

library tumbling, the exterminator's bill. Rapacious bugs devour,
a red flag calls up the poem: Blood. Zinnia. Emergency. Blackbird's

vermillion epaulet. Crimson of manicure. Large red man reading,
handkerchief red as a clitoris peeking from his deep tweed pocket—

Suddenly he was gone, gold draining from the walls, but the leaf,
the leaf was in my hand, and in the silence I heard an engine howl,

and through the night that darkened behind the window, I saw
light bolt forward, the tail of a comet smudge black winter sky.

GNOSTIC

When I wake up, I can remember touching the back of your neck, the cut of your hair blunt under my fingers.

In the dream you have met my mother. My sisters and I are living in a grand house where I have no room of my own.

One of my sisters has delineated her property by stringing a rope from which she will hang photographs of our dead father.

At the beginning of Christianity, a bishop established what is called the "canon of truth" in order to unify feuding believers into a single way of apprehending the sacred. His teachings excluded the workings of imagination as subjective, vulnerable to self-interest, and possibly insane.

Your neck, the blunt cut of your hair sharp and fragrant on my fingers.

You come to the big house, you have just met my mother at a party where curtains of royal blue fell to the floor. The music by Scarlatti.

My hair is turning gray.

I look in the mirror. The familiar dark hairs are fine and smooth, the white are rough and thick like the fiber of which clouds are woven. I want to pluck out the white hairs, but my tweezer falls through them like logic through the sense of dreams.

I am getting old, soon it will be too late. Your hand will slide from my skin like silk falling from a polished table.

In the big house you come to me, and I show you my rectangle of floor. It is here I will put my couch and desk, separated from my sister and her pictures of our dead father by the edges of my body, myself, my thinking.

You consider me. We stand there for a while.

My sister is attaching the large photographs of our father to a rope.

I look into the mirror at my white hair. I have sworn I will never dye it, but now I must. The white hairs are growing as fast as snow falls across a landscape. Soon snow will obliterate the town and countryside, there will be no houses visible, cars will disappear under the mass of it, trees will become poignant marks on a dangerous blank.

My sister strings photographs of our dead father along the rope, attaching them with small invisible clips.

I wait for you.

I think about your face, how you are becoming bald, and then I remember touching you for the first time, the back of your neck. I was wondering how to find you, what I would discover there. It made me almost cry that you stayed perfectly still, certain, it seemed, that what I was imparting was of utmost consequence. I moved my fingers tentatively, as if finding first knowledge in a terrain I could slip beneath, into a garden.

I remembered that when I woke up. That and your sticky skin.

Certain early Christian ideologues denigrated imagination as outside the realms of good and evil. My mother is no longer dead, and you have met her. The air is transparent, the colors dark wood and pale amber.

I am standing at the mirror watching white hair grow in as fast as snow.

What time is the train coming?

You sit at the window, your legs crossed. Courtly and at ease, you scrutinize my face until I am self-conscious.

I become aware that you are waiting for me. I don't know how to get to you.

Some early Christians, those who came to be persecuted as heretics, believed that a part of God is perpetually hidden from us. In relation to that realm of the deity dwells imagination, unceasingly seeking understanding of what is concealed.

I can see you on the window seat in an elegantly cut suit, as if wearing such clothes were a form of grace.

I remember you in that suit, standing in the hotel, turning on your heel to look for me. Now the window is tall behind you, twilight gathering outside the glass, cedars black beyond the roses.

I am not dead, yet I am mute as the dead usually are in dreams. You are speaking in a clear voice, explaining you have met my mother and that I look like her.

Before sleep, I was reading about early Christianity. When I woke up from the long dream, there we were in the taxicab, my arms tentative around you, my fingers seeking the back of your neck.

I felt clearly the blunt edge of your newly cut hair, the stickiness of your skin, that mortal stickiness—

When my mother's mother was sixty, her hair was still dark. When my mother died at fifty, her hair was still black, though as she sickened, it turned white, black receding as life did.

I stand at the mirror, its rare wide-beveled glass framed by oak carved to leaves and flowers. I am scrutinizing myself. My face is not ageing, but my hair is turning white, cloaking the trees, falling on the meadow, windblown across the frozen lake. What heresy is it that you come to me in a dream, knowing everything?

The tall windows rise to the ceiling, but I don't lift my eyes. I don't want to lose sight of you.

Outside, the cedars. Beyond them a smooth body of water.

III

B E A U T É

Inge Morath, 1923–2002
Arthur Miller, 1915–2005

NIGHT

As if his hands could claw away her death
on this wide table in the dark

city outside, windows lit or not lit, the sheet
a shroud for my living body

and she is in me begging to come back
Nothing will bring her back

after we left she lay there, only body
and then for three days they burned her

the living husband pounding the table
water, she says, mouth begging

as if his hands were the claws of her absence
Nothing will bring her back

and she is in me breathing
from the metal bed, the husband near

thirsty, she says, a chip of ice from the white bowl
to push onto her tongue

Or outdoors, all of us at the table
breeze noisy in the locust, lettuce in the red bowl

and she passes the blue glass pitcher
There was an elm here once

the husband tilting his fork as he speaks
and we are suddenly attentive

knives left on the magnet, one hand
on the other chopping

oil hot in the black skillet *Darling will you
cut the parsley?* and hands me scissors.

BEAUTÉ

The voice was accented by her first language,
German as spoken in Austria (she was from Graz).

She did not hand me the parsley, she gave me scissors
and sent me outdoors. This happened all the years

I went there—either I would cut mint from the garden
or parsley, or chives. She made salad in a huge tin bowl,

red on the outside and white on the inside
with a black rim, or if there were only a few of us

she used a smaller bowl of transparent Plexiglas.
Cutting parsley meant stumbling into the night,

out sliding doors into the dusk or the dark.
I was always nervous I wouldn't cut the right

amount of parsley or mint. I came in through
the kitchen. When I arrived, she would turn from

the stove or sink, say my name in her accent, embrace me,
and pulling back to look at me, say "Beauté!"

Even though I had studied French, it took years
to understand she was saying "beauty," though

I knew somehow when she said that word, she was
making new life for me. When she said "Beauté."

those syllables were light and I was in that light.
I use the word "stumbled" because I was so

self-conscious. If I cut the parsley as she wanted
then, I reasoned, she would smile again, exclaim

that word I didn't understand and send me
to the room where guests were or just her husband

watching the news, turning it off when he saw me,
offering his cheek for a kiss. She spoke seven languages—

German, also French, Romanian (in Bucharest,
nineteen when she left Berlin to study there),

English (the first husband, British, married to become
"Madame" to live "as I pleased" which she did after

the immediate divorce), Spanish (fifty years of
photographing—flamenco, matador, a village

that gave a street her name). When her daughter was a child,
she studied Russian to read the poems. In her fifties

she learned Chinese. Near eighty, photographing
Styria, in Slovenia, the place her mother's

family had always lived—*How are the pictures?*
She collapsed on that trip. *From pain.* Yet continued

photographing. *Because it was important.* The proofs
on her sickbed. Reaching for the pill bottle—

Darling, will you hand me those? Lifting one leg
to divert pain. *How are the pictures? Very*

interesting, she said, though forthrightly
modest. And we talked about what pain allows.

When I met her I was thirty-nine,
though now I'm no younger than she was

the day she came to take the first portrait.

STYRIA

And mountains blackening, then also gray, transparent, the clouds
cumulus, undersheathed with darkness. Did you understand walking
summer's departure

would come so black? Yellow greens of August grassland, further
mountains cerulean, lavender, indigo, and you, legs
in those narrow jeans,

frayed bag across your shoulder, camera to an avid eye.
What I understand now I saw later, after you burned greens
charcoal in the dark:

It looks like an edge of the earth, a place love would not interrupt
thought, the hot sphere of pain already inscribing its purpose
up your spine, climbing

into your seeing, but you stride forward, behold suddenly
the serenity in rest, something you gave but did not take.
For you, always, rest

was, if not waste, unnecessary. So much of your thinking
inhabited seeing—why stop looking? And what is this falling,
tilting of meadow

but an idea of the next place? Understanding one dimension
inclines us toward another—the field where you walked as a girl,
your mother suntanned

and your brother. Here, now, are those afternoons, a meadow
become alternation of density, a deft beckoning
of intimation,

all green but gray in the photograph, shadows of conifer
striping, sloping, narrow then widen. Solidifying as if all
foreground were darkness.

Afternoon

Before he turned to leave
she gazed at the height of him

I was rubbing her foot
its heat back

Do you have your keys, darling?
and he was gone

If I had known, I would have stayed
He leaned to kiss her

and she lifted herself toward him
I could swear her feet were blue

We were carrying her down
corridors, my long narrow

dream, the husband walking
with difficulty, enough light so I could see—

older, he waited for the bus
with flowers

she became a purposeful bird
feeding him, beloved

toward the waiting car
so that from the kitchen I could hear him

shout my name, so that when I went out
the driver with pink shiny skin

smiling, opened the door
her weakness flung her

across the seat
I stood lifting my hand

to the moving glass
through the moving glass I could see

as the car turned
her open hand dive from view

ALIVE

The last I saw her alive was in the apartment. Not the last time ever
but the last time *alive*—that is, so we could have a conversation.

Oh darling, I'm not well, quick exhale on the telephone. As always
I dressed for her, but also grabbed poems. You should understand

beneath the leap to a taxi, magenta raw silk, was a pull downward—
in private I called it "not a good feeling." She was on the sofa, pale

scarf around her head. I kissed her—nervous, self-consciousness
I'd felt those years ago stumbling into the dusk with scissors.

Her husband had to go out, and when I got there, was already
putting on his tweed jacket, cap, standing, his back to us

at the window. His face must have shown dread, which was why
in addition to age, his hands were fumbling on the table

as if he were blind. That was when I saw across her face
such love for him it rose in me. *Do you have your keys, darling?*

He turned, reluctant, and leaned to kiss her, delicate as a boy
bowing at dancing school, and she, ignoring the pain,

lifted herself toward him, all her beauty in the reach
strength still allowed. Door closing behind him. The wall of chalk

making itself complete. *Sit over there*, she said, *so I can
look at you.* And I moved across the room.

There's so much I want to ask you, I said. She just looked at me.
She didn't shrug, though I felt that sort of resignation in her gaze.

I wanted to ask about her life as a woman, hear stories again
I had faint memories of—the long-ago lover she saw by chance once

in her sixties on a boat. I had expected years of time
and now, believing I would not have those years, every question

vanishing, I looked at that changed familiar face. Was it I who
was so blank? I picked up poems, leafed through. In her twenties

in Vienna, she had known Ingeborg Bachmann, and always for her
a poem was a talisman. Emily Dickinson, I said, and began reading.

Though I chose at random, every poem delineated circumstances
in which my friend now found herself—and I was embarrassed:

Why should the living proclaim hard truths to the dying?
And yet I could not stop reading, in part because the knowledge

forming itself between us had through it the dangerous vulnerability
of love. *It's a miracle*, she said, as if relieved to come to understandings

she'd long struggled for. After I'd read, grasping as if the poems were
handrails at the edge of something I did not want to enter, she said,

What about yours? And so I read one in which cool water replaces
disabling pain, and one in the voice of a Degas bather. I did not read

the poem dreaming Paul's death; I did not want death in that room.
In the kitchen, I heated her some miso soup. *Sit down, darling.* And

reaching her too-thin arm, she pulled from the cushions behind her
a tiny silver camera, not her Leica but a digital, and lifted it

to her eye. *Oh that's beautiful*, she said. *Will you adjust the light?*
And squeezed the button over and over, my undying body

big and clumsy. You'll go to the country tomorrow? *Yes,
I want fresh air.* Outside, evening was darkening the gray

church walls as in the silence we watched pigeons slowly wheel
in winter sky. I put my coat on, touched her arm, leaned to kiss her,

the distant shouts of children leaving school across the street.

WINDOWS

Before weakness comes to my hands
as they warn it will

before it roughens the skin
let me reach and pull it back

without the clouding in of all our mistakes
this would be heaven

she turns her face and these rooms too
are filled with light

instead of that door, there is no door
instead of a dark room

there are rooms of transparent light
of light that has no color

then sunrise burns window frames
orange, glass suddenly blue

"emptiness" the lake says
or "this is the skin of another world"

and "nakedness"
as if the hand he slid into me

actually made flesh a river
and darkness light,

a sculptor's hand twisting
until the drowning is to his liking

this brought me to my knees
and it was God I shouted for.

PORTRAIT

When I sat down, my hands felt impossible. *Just fold them,*
she said, looking, pressing the button, shifting the angle,

pressing again. The portrait is black and white, the settee
blue and orange, behind me a corner of my grandmother's

self-portrait. I thought I looked old, but, gesturing as if
smoothing a tablecloth, she said, *Your face has an asymmetry*

I like. We met at the house of a dancer, they were all friends
so I was quiet, near her husband at the round table. It was June,

and how do I remember this? We had London broil, cooled
to room temperature. When I noticed raspberry on my shirt,

she and her husband were telling a story—Cambodia, escaping
to Laos as the Vietnamese advanced, she had photographed

Angkor Wat, the daughter a child, airport closed, crossing
borders in the rain forest. I watched her, long fingers moving

in failing light, framing the air with stretched hands. Might she
photograph me? She arrived in the morning. From my open door,

watching her leap from the car, flimsy red camera bag, jeans, shirt
rolled to the forearm, the quick suggestion I sit, fingers

adjusting the lens, her icon face in March light. You'll see
sorrow in my eyes in the one she chose. In the dining room,

she asked me to stand against the wall, camera sliding
across her face. Was I working? Was I happy? As if to work

was to be happy. In Paris, she photographed Cocteau, Picasso;
in Russia, Nadezhda Mandelstam, in New York, elsewhere,

so many my portrait traveled with, hair messily piled, broken
hair stick, eyes sorrowful, to Barcelona, Vienna, Paris . . .

Night after night, they invited me to supper. *We thought
you seemed a little lost.* I gave her precise gifts, and she,

scorning the purchased, gave things she had—the string of
Egyptian beads, a sea-blue scarab, a silver hand, the mandala

on rice paper. Last Christmas Eve, pale scarf already wrapping
her head, I opened her presents, the book about saints, a walnut

carved with tiny faces of the Buddha. I waited to open
the flat box, leaning close to keep her warm, almost reluctantly

lifting the lid, my younger eyes shocking my present ones to tears
It's how you looked then. Then? When had that March day

ceased to be part of now? Through the Christmas supper she was
too weak to cook, we sat, dancer, daughter, husband, beloveds,

as if by humbly enacting this night, we might forestall what was,
have back that summer I was lost and they found me, equinox

sky bright, the three of us cavorting, wide lawn blackening
at the edge of the entire earth, dark falling like a spangled veil.

CORRIDOR

She has her hands in the pockets
of her pale sweater. She gazes out,
hair pulled back into shadow.
Her double stands in the closed
compartment, but because daylight
can't hit the glass, seems to wait
quiet in the dark, an earlier woman
who makes this journey often,
knows the train, what route it takes
across this shifting border.

Through the window, the girl sees
two, three sets of tracks, frazzle
of hillock, house so quickly passing
it could be just a dream. Bright
things are so white in the photograph
she seems lit from within,
numinous—the train thrumming
door handle, door handle, door—
hanging lights streaky in the dimness
hiving the barrel ceiling.

It was morning you asked her
to face the window, bend her left arm
at that loose angle, position

hands in pockets as you might have
in 1945, having survived the war
to watch where you were going
come closer and closer, to leave
behind that border a future
unchosen, locked away
inside what never happened.

DREAM

Appointed to die
among the others, I waited

It is a privilege
to pass into the land of the dead

without suffering
and so I did not protest

was lowered
shovelfuls of dirt thrown

thunder of entire burial
I could see daylight

through a hole in the coffin lid
door cracked

opening at the head of a cave
daylight, white of winter daylight

apparently I was not dead
not dead, shouting

breathing not dead yet
banging, banging from the inside

of death, the lid of death
with undead fists

Her likeness plastered
colorful kiosks along the Ring

near the Opera House, the great hotels
across the terrace at lunch

her beautiful friends
a woman with white hair cut to her chin

Haben Sie sie gesehen?
the woman wearing bright silk

from Milan, the tall one
known since they were girls

Erkennen Sie diese Person?
in German, Where is she?

banging, banging from inside
this daylight death

banging out of breath
shovel hitting

I can see them digging
the box lifted, death opened

faces, cold sky
headstones almost white

the air white
myself stepping from the coffin in black clothes

indifferent observers
incompetent diggers, as if wise

to my unearned death
had buried me shallow.

Music

The husband leading us
to the water

even the black we wore was bright
moving across blond grass

afternoon unseasonable, warm
darkness already present

but also the feel of spring
in weeks the first daffodils

that first summer after swimming
she would send me upstairs—

There are clean towels, darling

his hand at the window latch
and she is lying there

one leg then the other perpendicular
her face telling

the pain, unbearable
as if such bodily insistence must be answered

with relief
at the broken latch his hand

his mouth set
against telling the private

So much of what I did was to please her

and when the moment comes
the gesture is abrupt, ceremonial

at the edge of the black water
his great arm bending

elbow rising in gray air
he holds the wooden box

he digs for ash as if for food
(the hunger was sadness)

And then, arm lifting, his hand
opened to the sky

and what she had burned to
rose, taking the light.

Porcelain

In the barn where the funeral would be held, we unpacked flowers
her daughter and I quiet, pulling blooms from tissue and plastic, bringing

vases from the house, the Meissen that survived bombardment,
as she told it: front wall sheared from the house, a young woman

walking toward home, evidence she had escaped death coming into view,
the vase, porcelain, gilt, magisterial, prevailing on a table, peculiar

and small in the daylight. *I want you to know*, vowels of her accent
at dinner, tears glassing her eyes. First a stem of white stock, then

of Lancelot delphinium, the near-blue rose and white; Austrian friends
hanging her photographs, whispering; the tall assistant framing

portraits of her—as girl, young woman, mother with husband, child,
an arrangement now depicting finality rather than continuance.

Though she gave me every love a daughter might ask, I was not
her daughter, and the hours before the funeral I turned away, chagrined

in the face of the solemnity with which the daughter crossed the room
where she had once made paintings, her mother at work, alive

not yards away. Crossed, holding with both hands the vase, her face intent. On the arrangement of chairs and flowers? Or on the invisible

now becoming presence, the woman who had died, her body now ashes in a box cut from wood. Turned toward the window to place flowers

so her mother will be here, absence enveloping like presence, lack now familiar, recognized. As loving, we could vainly hope, as our friend.

GLOVES

One long-fingered hand strokes
the other chemo-scoured wrist

as if pulling on an evening glove
pulling off rubber gloves at the sink

I met one of my old lovers in Paris.
He said he never imagined

I would have kitchen hands, and now these.
Yellow rubber, wet with dishwater

After a while the body is not so pretty
Sheets bright as mirrors

she turns in her last bed, but I remember
grass under bare feet

running toward the pond
we carry our towels.

Why did you marry?
I wanted to live with him.

You should have seen her smile
It broke darkness in two.

ADVICE

I want to tell her the hotel kiss

glass doors spinning us onto the avenue,
watching him spear honeydew, green

vanishes into his mouth, how as the waiter spoke
he fingered my silked upper arm

until my mouth broke composure.
"He's married," was all I said.

She tells: Ionesco for supper at her "flat"
Saul Steinberg, also Rumanian,

and the writer she will marry.
She cooks "something simple," a blizzard,

they drink and laugh, lights go out,
drive uptown in the snow, the writer's

Jaguar "miraculously" unaffected,
Rumanian conversation, her abrupt trip

to Paris when the writer hedges,
then he follows her.

She scrutinizes my face,
He's married. . . .

shrugs as if conjugal circumstance
were immaterial.

"As long as you don't hurt anyone on purpose,"
as hearing her husband on the stairs

she turns her eyes toward him.

PILGRIMAGE

I dream of that winter

hospital room, her face jangling
toward me, asking for ice

but the season hesitates
and something confuses the clock hands

as she extends her toes
as she bends her arms and reaches

as color comes back into the bedclothes
as we begin to talk

first in monosyllables about her condition
then in sentences that rise and fall

like sentences the living speak

I have missed you, I say
and get that fast, urgent smile

I want to tell her about Christoph
how he made me laugh with his stories

Josef on a tricycle in the desert
riding to mass in Cairo when they were young

but I'm not sure there's time

now her fingers are warm, she is curling
and uncurling them

recognition in her face
metal of the bed becoming wood

she is sitting up, speaking

she has climbed a mountain in a blizzard
her feet cursing the difficulty of it

as with others she reaches
the summit where a cross is dug into the ground

where the small church is

it was hard, she says, it snowed every day
and it was cold.

WRISTS

Who but God's hand
could turn a body to light

the shard of ice to water in her mouth?

I wanted to touch her
but these were the hours of argument

What is she made of?
Who does she belong to?

hours of proof the body is no more
than wood or leaf or stone

She had become something of His

as when the man split me with his hand
boulders pushed aside

as in a full river
earth becomes mud, and then nothing

or clouds withdraw at evening, leaving
radiance and then blue

I became nothing

plums on her kitchen table
the black-and-white floor

I do not mean the man himself
was God

or even that God moved through his hand

afterward I was standing
and as I bent he told me to bend further

Imagine you're running downhill
he was holding my wrists

and as I bent further I began to weep

my body lurching
until there was no word for it

RED SHOES

all that autumn you step from the train

as if something were burning

something is burning

running across green grass bare feet

that day death was only

what we lose in fall comes back in spring

something is burning

from the train you climb

smoke between the skyscrapers

Paris was so beautiful, the sky—

all that autumn

then tears

Why do we do this again?

she turns to you in the kitchen

she puts her arms around you

she is wearing those red shoes

Violetta, 2000: Violetta is the name of the courtesan in Verdi's *La Traviata* (1853), taken from the novel by Alexandre Dumas, *fils*, (later a play) *La Dame Aux Camelias* (1848), which in turn was based on the actual life of his mistress, the courtesan, Marie Duplessis (1824–1847).

Gnostic: The book about early Christianity: Elaine Pagels, *Beyond Belief* (2003).

Wallace Stevens: "Large Red Man Reading" is the title of a poem by Wallace Stevens.

Beauté: Inge Morath's photographs are collected in *Inge Morath: Fotografien 1952–1992* (Edition Fotohof im Otto Müller Verlag, Salzburg 1992) and elsewhere.

Styria: After a photograph by Inge Morath, 2001.

Alive: Ingeborg Bachmann (1926–1973), Austrian poet, dramatist, and novelist. Honor Moore poems "Darling," "Shoulder," and "She Remembers" in *Darling* (2001).

Portrait: This and others of Inge Morath's portraits are collected in *Portraits* (Aperture, 1986). Nadezhda Mandelstam (1899–1980), wife of poet Osip Mandelstam (1891–1938) and author of two memoirs, *Hope Against Hope* and *Hope Abandoned*. After her husband was killed in the Soviet Gulag, she kept his works alive by memorizing them.

Corridor: After a photograph by Inge Morath, 2001.

Dream: *Haben Sie sie gesehen?* (Have you seen her?) *Erkennen Sie diese Person?* (Do you recognize this person?)

Pilgrimage: Inge Morath walked the Camiño Santiago in Spain. Her photographs of the pilgrimage are collected *Camiño de Santiago/Inge Morath* (Universidad de Santiago de Compostela, 1999).

ACKNOWLEDGMENTS

Beauté (the sequence) is for those around the table in Roxbury.

Thank you to the friends and colleagues who read and commented on the manuscript, in particular Carolyn Forché, Donna Masini, Victoria Redel, Lynn Emanuel, Richard Matthews, and, not least, Joanna Klink. For their contributions to the composition of *Beauté* (the sequence), I am grateful to John Jacob of the Estate of Inge Morath, Werner Mörath, Julia Bolus, Christoph Meran, and Mary Ann Camilleri.

For residencies while writing this book, my enduring gratitude to the Corporation of Yaddo, The MacDowell Colony, and Medway Plantation (Bokara Legendre). For their hospitality, I am also grateful to Ellen Kuras, Marian Moore, Rebecca Miller, Barbara Kassel, Judith Thurman, Barbara Maltby and Michael Janeway, Wendy Gimbel and Doug Liebhafsky, and Claudia Weill and Walter Teller.

Thanks as always to Sarah Chalfant, and to Jill Bialosky, Evan Carver, Jo Anne Metsch, and everyone at W. W. Norton.

Thank you, too, to the editors of publications where some of these poems appeared, sometimes in a slightly different form:
Bloom: "Music"
Bomb: "Styria," "Portrait," "Pilgrimage"
Boston Review: "Disparu," "Corridor"
Jubilat: "Blues from Bed"
Lit: "Summer," "New Shoes"
Open City: "Tango," "Hotel Brindisi," "Homage"
Salmagundi: "Gnostic," "Violetta, 2000," "Wallace Stevens"